THE
PORCUPINE

BY
CARL R. GREEN
WILLIAM R. SANFORD

DISCARD

EDITED BY
DR. HOWARD SCHROEDER
**Professor in Reading and Language Arts
Dept. of Elementary Education
Mankato State University**

PRODUCED AND DESIGNED BY
BAKER STREET PRODUCTIONS
Mankato, MN

CRESTWOOD HOUSE

Mankato, M

CIP

LIBRARY OF CONGRESS CATALOGING IN PUBLICATION DATA
Sanford, William R. (William Reynolds)
 The porcupine.

 SUMMARY: Describes porcupines, their life cycle, their characteristics,
the dangers of their world, and their possibilities as pets.
 1. Porcupines--Juvenile literature. (1. Porcupines) I. Green, Carl R. II.
Title.
QL737.R652S26   1985   599.32'34   85-7899
ISBN 0-89686-280-1 (lib. bdg.)

International Standard Book Number:	Library of Congress Catalog Card Number:
0-89686-280-1	85-7899

CRESTWOOD HOUSE

Hwy. 66 South, Box 3427
Mankato, MN 56002-3427

TABLE OF CONTENTS

INTRODUCTION:

Friday, May 13th

Dear Diary:
Talk about unlucky Fridays!

My dog Rex met his first porcupine today. I don't think he will ever forget it. The porcupine? It didn't seem upset. The little critter taught Rex a good lesson. Then it walked away.

Anyway, here's what happened. I took Rex for a walk in the woods. The sun was out and it was a warm, breezy day. Rex ran around in circles, happy as can be.

I saw the porcupine first. It was walking along as if it owned the woods. Of course, I stopped to watch. It looked like a walking pincushion. The "pins" were hundreds (thousands?) of sharp quills. I know now that scientists call these eastern porcupines *Erethizon dorsatum.* Western porcupines are named *Erethizon epixanthum.* Dr. Taylor told me that. She comes into the story later on.

As I was watching ol' Quilly, Rex came running up. The porcupine must have heard him. Quilly growled, arched its back, and rattled its quills. Those quills were standing up like needles! But that didn't stop Rex. He dashed in, ready to take a big bite.

4

Quilly's tail lashed up like a whip. That tail full of quills hit Rex right in the face.

The fight was over right then. Rex howled like he was dying. At least thirty quills were sticking out of his mouth. I picked him up and carried him home. Mom took us to Dr. Taylor. She's an animal doctor — a veterinarian.

This dog shows what can happen during a fight with a porcupine.

Dr. Taylor put Rex to sleep for awhile. Then she started taking the quills out. The quills have little barbs at the end and are hard to pull out. Left alone, the quills might have worked their way to Rex's brain. That would have killed him!

Dr. Taylor told me about porcupines. Their name really means "quill pig." It comes from the Latin *porcus* (for pig) and the French *epine* (for thorn or quill). Porcupines aren't pigs, though. They're big rodents. That's the same family as rats and gophers. In North America, the beaver is the only rodent that's bigger than a porcupine.

Well, I hope Rex has learned his lesson. I'm not sure if he has. Dr. Taylor says dogs are slow learners when it comes to porcupines. She also told me that most wild animals have learned to leave porcupines alone. That makes good sense. I know I don't want to get close to those sharp quills!

That's all for now. I have to go take care of Rex.

Most wild animals leave porcupines alone. This close-up photo of quills shows why!

CHAPTER ONE:

Most people know one fact about porcupines: These unusual rodents defend themselves with sharp quills.

Is that a myth? No. The average adult porcupine has about thirty thousand quills. That's over one hundred quills per square inch (15 per square cm)! These needle-sharp quills cover most of the animal's body. The tail alone has over two thousand quills. The mature quills are loosely attached to the skin. They come out easily when the porcupine is attacked. When that happens, new quills replace the ones that are lost. They grow to their full length in two to six months.

The shortest quills are about half an inch (1.3 cm) long. These tiny quills grow around the porcupine's cheeks. The longest quills grow on the sides and top of the tail. These quills grow to about three inches (7.6 cm) in length. No quills grow on the porcupine's furry underside. This unprotected area runs from the chin to the tip of the tail.

Why is a quill so deadly?

Quills are actually modified hairs. Each quill is hollow for most of its length, but the tip and the base are solid. The upper half is hard and black. The tips are needle sharp. They go through skin easily, almost without pain.

In addition, each quill has fine scales at the end. These tiny "barbs" are so small you'd need a magnifying glass to see them. The scales spread out after the quill enters the victim's skin. This holds the quills in place. After that, they start working their way into the victim's body. Natural movements of the body work the quills inward as fast as an inch (2.5 cm) per day!

One of the oldest of all myths says that porcupines throw their quills. People have imagined the quills flying like arrows. But that is not true. Once in awhile, a loose quill does fly a few feet when a porcupine slaps its tail. But these "flying" quills probably wouldn't stick in your skin.

Imagine a hungry predator taking a swat at a porcupine. It's likely to pull back a paw full of quills. The quills hurt, but they're not poisonous. In fact, recent studies have shown that the quills carry their own mild antibiotic. That's why they seldom cause an infection. But they're hard to get out. Humans can pull them out with pliers. Animals have a harder time of it.

Wounded animals rub at the quills. This tends to drive the quills deeper. If the quills reach a vital part of the body, they can kill the animal. There's another danger as well. An animal with a mouth full of quills

The quills of a porcupine can kill animals of all sizes.

cannot eat. It may die of hunger. Quills have killed animals of all sizes. The list includes wolves, mountain lions, bears, and eagles.

Quills aren't always dangerous

You can safely pet a tame porcupine. Just be sure to move your hand from the head backwards. The quills will lie flat, covered by soft guard hairs. But don't alarm the porcupine! If you do, the animal will raise its quills. It has a layer of strong muscles under the skin. When it tightens the muscles, the quills stand up.

Despite this danger, Indian hunters once caught porcupines with their bare hands! The trick was to grab the porcupine's tail from below. The fingers then curled upward and held down the quills on top of the tail. After that, it was simple to drop the porcupine into a sack. The Indians ate the meat and used the quills to decorate baskets, moccasins, and war bonnets.

Quills also serve as a "life jacket" for the porcupine. The quills are filled with air. They help keep the porcupine afloat in water. This is useful, because porcupines sometimes feed on water lilies and other water plants. That's why you might see them swimming in a pond or lake.

Adapted to a life with quills

Living with thirty thousand quills doesn't bother the porcupine. For example, porcupines mate in the usual way. The female just keeps her quills flat while the male is standing over her. Giving birth is not a problem, either. Newborn porcupines are born in a sac, like many other mammals.

Newborn porcupines, called porcupettes, have fewer quills than the adults. The quills are soft when the porcupette is born. The quills harden quickly, however. Even newborn porcupines know how to defend themselves! A porcupette will arch its back and lash out with its tail. They know how to do this by instinct.

There's much more to porcupines than quills, however. So let's find out more about nature's "pincushions."

The quills stand up when the porcupine tightens its back muscles.

11

CHAPTER TWO:

Porcupines can be found in many parts of the world. They live in the woodlands and forests of Europe, Africa, Asia, South America, Central America, and North America.

Long ago, North America's porcupines came north from South America. They made themselves at home in almost any wooded area. Today, their range extends from Texas to Alaska, and across most of Canada. They are also found in the northeastern U.S., from Maine to Virginia. Some people call them hedgehogs. That's a mistake. The European hedgehog is a very different animal.

A stay-at-home animal

Porcupines prefer habitats with plenty of trees. Some are also found in scrub-desert areas. Wherever they live, porcupines are not great travelers. A typical range covers only ten to thirty acres. Within that area, porcupines live by themselves. The porcupettes stay with their mothers for about six months. Then they move to a new area. As adults, they'll seek out other porcupines only during the mating season.

The porcupine's lonely life makes it seem as though it's a grumpy, bad-tempered animal. They're not. In fact, porcupines use their quills only for defense. The males fight with each other, but only when they're seeking a mate. Even then, the fights usually end without injury.

Porcupines need lots of trees in their habitats.

Varied sizes and colors

An adult porcupine is about the same size as a small dog. Their bodies range in length from twenty-six to thirty-four inches (66 to 86 cm). The tail adds another six to twelve inches (15 to 30.5 cm). A typical male weighs about fourteen pounds (6.4 kg). The smaller female weighs about eleven pounds (5.1 kg). A giant male might grow as large as forty pounds (18 kg). Males and females look very much alike.

Porcupines aren't large. They are about as big as a small dog.

People expect to see a porcupine's quills sticking out all the time. Instead, the quills are usually hidden under a coat of thick guard hairs. Eastern porcupines have brown or black guard hairs. The western porcupine is a lighter, more yellowish color. The longest guard hairs are often tipped with white. The summer coat is lighter and shinier than the winter coat.

Porcupines also have a thick coat of soft fur under the guard hairs. This wooly coat, along with the guard hairs, protects the porcupine during cold weather. They need the extra warmth. Porcupines may be forced to stay up in a tree for days at a time if the winter weather is bad.

Poor eyes, good ears and nose

Porcupines can see motion, but they can't see distant objects well. To make up for that, they have good hearing and a keen sense of smell. The smallest sounds and smells alert the porcupine to danger. That keen nose also helps porcupines find food, as well as other porcupines during the mating season.

All porcupines have a strong body odor. Some people say they smell like rotting wood. But porcupines don't mind. Their odor lets other porcupines know they're around. That's important when they're looking for a mate!

A diet of bark and plants

If you pull a porcupine's lips back, you'll see four long, slightly curved teeth — two on top, and two on the bottom. These powerful cutting teeth are called incisors. They keep growing all during the animal's life. The orange-colored incisors grind against each other. This action keeps them sharp. It also keeps them from growing too long. Farther back in the mouth, the porcupine has molars for chewing.

A porcupine's teeth are suited to its diet. During the winter, they strip bark from trees. Their favorite trees are maple, pine, spruce, elm, and linden trees which have a low acid content. Adult porcupines can eat up to a pound of bark a day. They also eat pine needles.

Spring fills the woods with a porcupine's favorite foods. They love the sweet, protein-rich buds and leaves of growing trees. As the snow melts, they also feed on tender forest plants. In the summer, porcupines will steal a farmer's carrots, potatoes, corn and

This birch tree has been stripped of its bark by a porcupine.

other crops. Water plants are another favorite food.

The porcupine's normal diet is low on salt. This is a problem for people who live near porcupines. Anything a person touches will have a little salt left on it. Porcupines sniff out these objects. People have found axe handles, canoe paddles, boots, and saddles chewed to bits. Porcupines also chew on plywood because they like the taste of the glue that holds the layers together.

Porcupines do most of their feeding and moving around at night. That's why people don't usually see a porcupine unless it's been hit by a car along a road.

A porcupine takes a chance when crossing a road.

At home in the trees

A porcupine's short legs give it a different walk. The legs are set wide apart and bow outward. This makes porcupines rock from side to side as they waddle forward. At its fastest gallop, a porcupine moves at a slow two miles (3.2 km) per hour.

The porcupine climbs trees slowly, but steadily. It has four toes on each front foot and five toes on each hind foot. Strong, curved claws give the porcupine a good hold on the tree. It climbs carefully, testing its grip at each step.

The tail is also useful in climbing. Short, stiff hairs grow on the underside of the tail. As the porcupine climbs upward, these hairs act like spurs. They hook into the bark and help keep the porcupine from sliding back.

Heights don't bother the porcupines. People report that they've seen them in trees as high as sixty feet (18.3 meters) above the ground.

Neither stupid or clumsy

People who see a porcupine for the first time may think it's a stupid animal. Instead of running from an enemy, a porcupine raises its quills and waits.

That makes it look a little silly. But is it? As a matter of fact, only a few animals will attack a porcupine that is showing its quills. They know better!

Despite their slow ways, porcupines learn quickly. A naturalist reported seeing a porcupine fall off a tree branch. The animal never went out on that branch again. The naturalist also saw another porcupine back onto a thin branch. The branch bent slowly down to the ground, and the porcupine climbed off. After that, it always took the same "elevator" down from the tree.

If you watch a porcupine waddle through the forest, it looks clumsy and slow. But even though a porcupine isn't graceful, it has a way of getting to where it wants to go. Up in the trees, it's a super climber. It never moves until it has a firm grip with its strong paws. If necessary, a porcupine can hang from a tree branch by one sharp claw.

Porcupines don't spend all their lives in trees, however. In the fall, each adult male goes looking for a female. The porcupine's life cycle begins with that yearly quest for a mate.

CHAPTER THREE:

The porcupine's life span is about ten years in the wild. These years pass in a regular cycle. During most of the year, porcupines live a slow, quiet life. Fall changes that pattern.

Fall is a time for mating

Fall is a restless time for porcupines. They feel the cold winter closing in. It's time to seek out the last vegetables, apples, and nuts. When the food is gone, they'll have to eat tree bark. Some porcupines look for a den. Others move down from the mountains to lower levels.

In the fall, some porcupines look for a den to use as a winter home.

In the late fall, porcupines become quite noisy. During the summer, a porcupine may go for weeks without making a sound. Only when it senses danger will it rattle its quills and grunt a warning. But these

When sensing danger, a porcupine will rattle its quills.

"silent" animals can also whine, bark, snort, and shriek. People have even heard them sob like a crying child. By November they are caught up in the mating urge. Both males and females sound off. The mating call is a whining "song" that varies with each animal.

The females grow more and more excited. They move around quite a bit, and chatter their teeth. The males set off to search for females. Males find the waiting females mainly by their odor. If males meet near a female, they may "wrestle" with each other. Fights are brief, however, and usually no one gets hurt. The winner tries to mate with the female.

Males climb the trees where the females are waiting. The females may or may not accept the first male who comes along. Once accepted, a male stays with the female for several days. The pair may touch paws and rub noses. Some even do a "love dance" on their back feet. After mating, the two separate. The male never comes back to help raise the porcupette.

Winter doesn't bother the porcupine

Porcupines often spend the winter in dens. Since they're not good diggers, they look for ready-made dens. Old badger holes, hollow trees, and rocky hillside caves are favorite spots. By keeping their quills down, porcupines can slip into tight spaces. Several porcupines might share a den, but they prefer to be alone. They often return to a good den year after year.

Porcupines are active all winter. They usually leave the den every day to eat. After the first snow, you will likely see porcupine tracks leading from a den to nearby trees. Porcupines aren't good at walking in deep snow, however. If the drifts are too deep, they may stay in a tree. During that time they feed on the bark. This habit gets them in trouble with foresters. If they strip off a circle of bark all around the trunk, the top of the tree will die.

Porcupines seldom starve. Tree bark is plentiful in the wooded areas where they live. Feeding porcupines also help other animals. Small branches drop to the ground as they gnaw on the tree. This provides food for rabbits, deer, and other grazing animals.

During the winter, porcupines lose most of the fat they built up in the summer and fall. As soon as the snow melts, porcupines leave their dens and winter trees. They go out in search of green plants, fruits, and grasses. They're hungry and must also replace the vitamins stored in their large livers. While feeding, they mark their territory with their strong scent — much like dogs do.

Porcupines will kill a tree when they eat the bark all around the trunk.

A female with its newly-born porcupette.

Spring brings new life

Females give birth to a single porcupette in April or May. Twin births are very rare. The female carries its young for seven months, which is a long time for a small mammal. Because of this long gestation period, porcupettes are well developed at birth. A newborn porcupine weighs about a pound (.5 kg), and measures about ten inches (25 cm) long. By comparison, a newborn black bear weighs only ten ounces (.28 kg).

The females need a safe place in which to give birth. Their tree-climbing days are over for a while. Favorite spots are in a hollow part of a fallen tree, under a tangle of bushes, or in a rocky den. The females make their choice with an eye on the nearby food supply.

The porcupette is born with its eyes open. It begins to nurse right away from the mother's four teats. A week or two later, it will start eating tender plants. The porcupette keeps on nursing for another four or five weeks. After about two weeks, however, a porcupette can survive on its own if the mother dies.

A tame three-week-old porcupette.

Young porcupines like to play. They toss sticks and pine cones around. If they meet another porcupette, they wrestle and gently bite each other. If a porcupette makes a squeaky cry for help, the mother usually ignores it. The young must learn to care for themselves.

Adult porcupines feed greedily on the spring's green plants. The fast-growing porcupettes have a tougher job. They must also master the lessons of survival.

A young porcupine must learn to find food, climb, and seek shelter. Most habitats provide a good supply of porcupine food. Each night, the young porcupines follow their mothers in search of food. They'll take much the same route the next night. Porcupines tend to be creatures of habit.

This is also a time to watch out for hungry enemies. The woods are full of predators who would like to eat a careless porcupine. In order to survive, porcupines must react quickly to the sounds and smells that mean danger.

Summer means activity

As the days go by, young porcupines grow more active and curious. Soon they'll be ready to go off on their own. The places where people have camped often attract them. They smell salt on everything humans have touched.

Wet weather doesn't seem to bother the porcupine. Rain or shine, it goes out to feed every night. Mosquitos are harder to ignore. Porcupines often climb a tree to get away from the pests.

Porcupines shed their wooly undercoat during the summer. That's not true of the quills, however. A porcupine without quills would be almost totally

In summer, porcupines lose their wooly undercoats. It's now easier to see their quills.

defenseless. Sometimes a few old quills might fall out when the porcupine shakes itself. But new quills grow constantly to replace those that are lost.

Porcupines become quite active in the late summer. The porcupettes have now moved away to be by themselves. Each porcupine begins to look for a winter den. They wander further each night in search of food. In early fall, adults begin to feel the mating urge.

The life cycle is about to begin again.

Porcupines eat more and more as fall approaches.

CHAPTER FOUR:

Unlike the family dog, wild animals usually leave porcupines alone. Those that don't, pay for their mistakes. Dead animals of all sizes have been found with quills in their bodies. Only a few predators regularly take the risk.

Fishers love a porcupine dinner

The fisher is one of the predators that hunts porcupines. Fishers are members of the weasel family. Quick and clever, they are about the size of a large house cat. They are very good at killing porcupines.

A drawing of a fisher.

A hungry fisher must first escape the porcupine's quills. It starts by jumping over the porcupine. That forces the porcupine to quickly turn its rear end toward the fisher. Then the fisher jumps again, and again, and again. This tactic tires the porcupine, as it tries to keep its quills pointed at the fisher. When the porcupine is finally worn out, the fisher darts in to bite the porcupine on the chin or neck, where it has no quills. The fisher may also reach in and flip the porcupine over, exposing its unprotected belly. Either way, the predator's sharp teeth soon kill its prey.

After the meal is over, scavengers move in to fight over the scraps. These "cleanup crews" include smaller animals, birds, and insects. When the scavengers finish, only the porcupine's pelt remains.

The fisher's meal is seldom totally free. Fishers have been found with dozens of painful quills in their bodies. If the quills reach a vital spot, the fisher will die, too.

Luckily for the porcupine, the fisher is not too common. Trappers have kept their numbers down. But good habitats for the fisher are found in Alaska, Canada, New England, and the Rocky Mountains. Foresters sometimes release fishers where porcupines are thought to be killing trees. The officials hope the fishers will go to work hunting porcupines.

Foresters sometimes release fishers when porcupines are thought to be killing to many trees.

33

Most predators are wary

Mountain lions, bobcats, coyotes, and weasels also hunt the porcupine. Among the winged predators, eagles and horned owls attack the porcupine.

Predators that hunt the porcupine tend to copy the fisher. That isn't as easy as it sounds, however. A porcupine keeps its quill-covered tail toward the enemy. The predator must be quick enough to get a

The porcupine's tail is covered will quills.

killing bite into an area not protected by quills. Coyotes solve the problem by working in pairs. When the porcupine lashes out at one coyote, the other runs in and knocks its victim over. Once it's on its back, the porcupine is fairly easy to kill.

However, porcupines often win these life-or-death fights. All of these predators have been found with quills in their bodies.

Sometimes a curious bear will touch a porcupine. When it does, a few quills stick in its paw. Angry now, the bear takes an even harder swing at the porcupine. You can guess the result of that bad choice!

Insects and parasites

Porcupines are bothered by insects and parasites. The bites of mosquitos, black flies, and gnats drive porcupines into the treetops. Ticks and lice live on the animal's skin. Other parasites, such as round-worms and tapeworms, live inside the porcupine's body. These parasites weaken the animal, but seldom kill it.

Porcupines also have their share of diseases and accidents. One deadly flu-like illness that kills porcupines is called "snuffles." Porcupines also die from tumors and tularemia fever. In addition, falls and scrapes can cause broken bones and infections. And a few unlucky porcupines even get stuck (and killed) by their own quills!

Humans are a threat

The porcupine's sharp teeth get it into trouble with people. Hungry porcupines damage trees, and farmer's crops.

Porcupines damage trees when they eat the bark. And they often feed on the same trees, year after year. The loss of bark and sapwood can kill branches, or even an entire tree.

Another type of damage comes when a snow-bound porcupine stays in the same tree. While feeding, it may eat a circle around the tree trunk. This kills the top of the tree. Not all of these "spike top" trees, however, are caused by porcupines. Many are caused by wind, lightning, and insects.

Foresters and farmers respond to the damage by trapping and poisoning porcupines. All too often though, these methods also kill other animals — and fail to control the porcupine.

Speeding cars kill many porcupines, too. These animals are often hit at night when they cross a road. The slow-moving porcupines can't move fast enough to get out of the way. However, the quills that can

A young porcupine sits on a "spike top."

kill a bear don't cause flat tires. Sharp as they are, the quills cannot work through rubber, leather, or other tough materials.

No protection from the law

Game laws regulate the hunting of many wild animals, but not the porcupine. They are thought of as "pests." Porcupines have been hunted since the days of the Indians. States with too many porcupines used to pay people to kill them. The payments were called bounties. Even the best bounty hunters couldn't find all the porcupines in a wooded area, however. As a result, some people cheated in order to collect the bounty money. For example, one state paid for each pair of porcupine ears turned in. A greedy bounty hunter could cut dozens of fake "ears" out of a porcupine's fur and collect a big payoff.

Despite all of these dangers, porcupines aren't likely to become extinct. They're usually hard to find in the daytime. You could walk though the woods for days, and never see one.

CHAPTER FIVE:

Wild animals belong in their natural habitat. But once in awhile, people find a young animal whose mother has been killed. A few families have raised porcupettes when this has happened.

Some families have made pets of porcupines.

Young porcupines can make good pets. They answer to their name and can learn simple tricks. But older porcupines do not adjust well to life as pets. They should not be taken home, even if they're injured and could be picked up.

Feeding pet porcupines is easy. They eat table scraps. They'll eat fruits, nuts, vegetables, and greens. But watch out! They'll also chew up the family's flowers, shoes, and the back steps!

Raising a porcupine

One family found a porcupette soon after it was born. Its mother had been killed by a car. They named it Porky. Porky was too young to eat solid food. At first, he refused the medicine droppers of milk. Then they put a mixture of honey, milk, and salt on his mouth. The porcupette licked its lips. Porky was soon sucking on a baby bottle full of milk.

Porky whimpered as though he missed his mother. His cries sounded like a human baby. That led to another idea. The family put a teddy bear and a heating pad in Porky's box. The tiny porcupine cuddled up to the teddy bear, and quit crying.

Playing with a porcupine

Porky grew quickly. Within a few weeks, he was crawling all over his owners. One flip of his tail could

Within a few weeks, porcupettes are climbing trees.

Pet porcupines can be very playful.

have filled them with sharp quills. But that never happened. Instead, Porky nipped playfully at their ears.

Like a cat, Porky liked to play with a ball. He also loved to have his stomach tickled. Next came the tricks. Porky learned to shake hands. Then he found a way to open his cage. Only a few animals could have learned new tricks faster.

Porky didn't mind being picked up by his front legs. He didn't let anyone pick him up by the tail, however. If someone grabbed his tail, he raised his quills. Too much handling also upset him. When he'd had enough, Porky went into hiding.

Porky smelled his food before eating it. If he liked it, he sat up on his hind legs. Then he would pick up the food with his front paws. Potato chips were Porky's favorite food.

It isn't all fun and games

At first it was fun to let Porky into the house. But that soon became a problem. He chewed on anything that people had touched. Pretty soon, most of the furniture was scarred by his sharp teeth. His strong body odor was also hard to take. And just when people were going to bed, Porky was ready to play. Like their wild cousins, pet porcupines are active at night.

As the months passed, Porky grew to full size. He weighed twenty-eight pounds (12.7 kg). As he grew older, he became less playful, and his owners built a "forest" cage for him. They covered the floor of the cage with branches. A large pan provided a water supply. They cut a small birch tree and put it in the corner. Porky climbed the tree like any wild porcupine. During the day he often slept on the cage floor.

Porky felt at home in his cage. If he didn't want to leave, it took two people to pry him loose. Pet porcupines seem to like people. They do not run away, even when they have a chance to do so. Perhaps life in the wild seems scary.

He wasn't a wild porcupine, but Porky followed the seasons. In the fall, he showed signs of wanting to mate. Later, on some winter days, he hardly moved at all. Once a day, he climbed down from his "tree" to eat and drink. Then he went back to his perch to wait out the cold weather.

Porcupines like Christmas

At Christmas time, one of the children let Porky into the house to see the tree. Porky knew what trees were for! He climbed into the branches. A child grabbed for him, but it was too late. Lights and colored balls flew in all directions.

By the time someone caught Porky, the tree was a mess. The porcupine's quills were covered with tinsel! But no one tried to punish Porky. How do you spank a porcupine?

Spanking a porcupine is out of the question.

MAP:

The shaded areas show most of the areas in North America that have porcupines.

INDEX/GLOSSARY:

47

WILDLIFE
HABITS & HABITAT

READ AND ENJOY THE SERIES:

If you would like to know more about all kinds of wildlife, you should take a look at the other books in this series.

You'll find books on bald eagles and other birds. Books on alligators and other reptiles. There are books about deer and other big-game animals. And there are books about sharks and other creatures that live in the ocean.

In all of the books you will learn that life in the wild is not easy. But you will also learn what people can do to help wildlife survive. So read on!